SCENES
of America

LOS ANGELES

SCENES

of America

LOS ANGELES

**JEFFREY SAMUDIO
AND PORTIA LEE**

Published by Arcadia Publishing
Charleston SC, Chicago IL, Portsmouth NH, San Francisco CA

Library of Congress control number: 2006920224

For all general information contact Arcadia Publishing at:
Telephone 843-853-2070
Fax 843-853-0044
E-mail sales@arcadiapublishing.com
For customer service and orders:
Toll-Free 1-888-313-2665

Visit us on the internet at www.arcadiapublishing.com

Unless otherwise noted, all images are courtesy of the Architectural Slide Collection of the University of Southern California.

CONTENTS

INTRODUCTION

This book records a community that established itself as it grew exponentially. Neither natural disasters nor financial losses daunted the first settlers or discouraged the new arrivals who sought the chance to begin again in a new city. Los Angeles city-makers had in mind an ideal city, and in its construction they demonstrated innovation and energy. In 1900, Los Angeles had been an American city for 50 years; in another 50 it would be a metropolis.

Los Angeles was founded in 1781 as one of the two original Spanish pueblos in California, entitling it to four square leagues of land. Set in a valley of the Los Angeles River, the pueblo was intended as a supply base for the garrisons of Southern California. Granted city status by the Mexican government in 1835, 60 years after its founding, the pueblo was still a small cattle market town surrounded by ranchos of immense acreage. The city began to reconsider its "cow town" condition in 1851, when statehood and the U.S. Board of Land Commissioners required it to prove its claims to city lands.

Los Angeles made a startling argument. It claimed not just four square leagues, but 16, as historian W. W. Robinson says, "longing even then to be the biggest city." The mayor and council attorneys argued that the law governing the establishment of the pueblo as four square leagues actually meant four leagues square, or 112 square miles. The city's argument did not prevail. Los Angeles's claim was denied and the city had to be content with its original grant.

The longing to be the biggest city did not go unrealized for long. Transcontinental rail service was established by 1881. New settlers required new land; new land required water. Los Angeles had prior rights to the waters that passed through the pueblo boundaries and it was willing to share it—with those inside its boundaries. The price of water for neighboring cities was annexation. First in were 904 acres on the former northeastern pueblo boundary; then the Shoestring Annexation of 1909 that brought Los Angeles its harbor. The Hollywood consolidation of 1910 brought population and the fledgling movie industry to a town that needed a sewer as well as water for households. By 1945, the small town that had begun with 28 square miles had grown to 450 through 95 annexations.

The images in this book document the buildings and community members of those eventful 50 years. Sometimes disappointed or unfairly cheated by circumstances, but always hard-working and resourceful, the citizens of Los Angeles built their communities. Businessmen constructed a downtown streetscape whose architecture excited envy in other cities. Hotels catered to visitors with such boosterism that they would go home, pack up, and return with sufficient capital for an ambitious scheme of their own. The introduction of the car into the mix allowed for mobility and a brand new outlook on life. Los Angeles became a drive-in city, laid out the freeway system, and decided not to ride on streetcars any more.

In a temperamental moment, Frank Lloyd Wright opined, "It's as if you tipped the United States up so that all the commonplace people slid down into Southern California." Perhaps they did slide down, but they hit the ground running too, intent on doing uncommon things in rather spectacular ways and looking sensational while it happened. From aqueducts to skyscrapers, the builders constructed the city that promised a place in the sun for everyone. The images of this book record journeys of a half-century—a short, bumpy, adventurous ride.

A NEW CENTURY

MOUNT LOWE RAILWAY CIRCULAR BRIDGE. Balloonist S. C. Lowe, whose profession precluded any fear of flight or heights, determined to share the thrill of aerial suspension with Angelenos. Hiring cable-car builder Andrew Hallidie, Lowe put into operation in 1893 the Great Incline to scale the foothills of the San Gabriel Mountains. The inaugural ascent on the Fourth of July brought passengers 1,500 feet from a pavilion in Rubio Canyon 2,000 feet above sea level with a 60 percent grade to the summit of Echo Mountain. After 127 curves and 18 trestles, the invigorated passengers arrived at the 5,000-foot summit which offered a restaurant, hotel, and cabins. The Circular Bridge, a tight curve of railway track, offered unparalleled views of Pasadena and Altadena, if the rider wasn't afraid to look. The rail line ran until 1938, although the facilities were destroyed earlier in fires and floods on the mountain.

LA GRANDE STATION, SANTA FE RAILWAY. The Moorish Revival style la Grande Station of the Santa Fe Railway opened with great fanfare on July 29, 1893. More than 50 trains daily departed from the station, which stood on Santa Fe Avenue between First and Second Streets. The main depot, 350 feet in length, had a central domed rotunda, tile floors, and a stained-glass window. An adjoining garden had a landscaped, kite-shaped walk and a miniature replica of the Santa Fe's excursion route to San Bernardino, planted in palms.

SAN PEDRO HARBOR. Los Angeles, situated on neither a navigable river nor the sea, created a harbor by dredging the mud flats and salt marshes of San Pedro Bay, 25 miles south of downtown. After 1910, when Wilmington and San Pedro were annexed to Los Angeles, the federal government and Los Angeles deepened channels, built breakwaters, and maintained a lighthouse at Point Fermin. This photograph, c. 1900, shows harbor construction using rock quarried from nearby Catalina Island.

15

THE HOLLENBECK HOTEL. The Hollenbeck was a prominent tourist hotel around the turn of the 20th century. It advertised to Eastern travelers through its climatic orientation, stating that most rooms faced east and south so that the early morning sun would warm rooms to a pleasant summer temperature even in winter. The Hollenbeck's bay windows and turrets were a city landmark until the structure was demolished in 1932.

LOS ANGELES CITY ENGINEER'S SURVEY TEAM. The City Engineers Survey Team stands in front of Old City Hall with the tools of their trade. The diversity of population in Los Angeles at the turn of the 20th century is evident in the faces of the workmen whose labors laid out the city's street grid and boundaries. (Archives of the City of Los Angeles.)

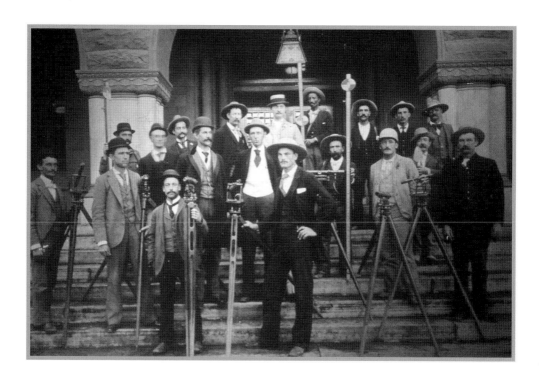

TROLLEY LINE AND POPPIES. This 1904 postcard celebrates the aromatic, bright orange state flower. These pleasure-seekers on the way to Mount Lowe rumbled out to the bright fields in the pristine countryside of the San Gabriel foothills.

OLD SEVENTH STREET TRESTLE BRIDGE. Old Seventh Street, an unsightly and flood-prone crossing, was swept away in the flood of 1905. It connected the main residential suburb of Boyle Heights, situated east of the river, with the downtown core of Los Angeles. (Collection of the Bureau of Engineering, City of Los Angeles.)

THE ANGELUS HOTEL, C. 1905. The Angelus Hotel had the characteristic style of an upscale downtown traveler's hotel. Wrought-iron balconies must have been welcomed by its visitors as a dramatic change from conventional stuffy rooms. An elaborate entrance provided another ornamental accent.

COURT FLIGHT, 1905. Located on Broadway between First and Temple Streets, Court Flight funicular raised passengers up the steep slope from Broadway to Court Street, just below the summit on Hill Street. Built in 1904, the facility burned in 1943.

OPPOSITE: INCLINE STATION, LOS ANGELES AND MOUNT WASHINGTON RAILWAY. Los Angeles and Mount Washington Railway built an attractive Mission Revival building at the Incline Station complete with refreshment bar for waiting passengers. The line continued upward to the Mount Washington Hotel, where visitors could stroll through the expansive gardens and enjoy a panoramic view.

SAN PEDRO HARBOR WITH SUBMARINES. In 1908 the Great White Fleet of the United States Navy anchored inside the partially completed breakwater of the port, bringing with them a small group of submarines. By 1912, the first section of the San Pedro Harbor breakwater was completed, the main channel widened and dredged to 30 feet.

PIGEON RANCH. Almost anywhere one looked in Los Angeles County in the early 20th century, some sort of agricultural enterprise was underway, and squab was in demand for banquets and fancy dinners. This Southern Pacific Coast Line railroad postcard allowed passengers to show those at home early California agribusiness.

31

HILL STREET TUNNEL, BUNKER HILL. Downtown Los Angeles topography was as opportunistic as the aims of its citizens. Sloping upward from the west bank of the Los Angeles River, the terrain presented a set of arroyos and rolling hills moving west from downtown. One of the most formidable geographic barriers was Bunker Hill. Continued progress westward was necessary, and by 1909, a tunnel had been bored through the hill.

THE ALEXANDRIA HOTEL. The Alexandria, the city's first fireproof class-A hotel, opened in 1906 and soon became a premier tourist destination. This postcard, with its American flags, banners flying, and massed band, indicates an important occasion, perhaps a presidential visit. This is certainly probable, since the Alexandria provided hospitality for Theodore Roosevelt, William Howard Taft, and Woodrow Wilson.

OPPOSITE: MARBLE LOBBY, ALEXANDRIA HOTEL. This c. 1910 postcard depicts the Alexandria's elaborate lobby. Unable to meet the competition as hotels moved west to more fashionable districts, the Alexandria's fame receded and it closed. Redecorated and modernized, it reopened in 1938. The lobby is still mostly intact.

CONSTRUCTION WORKERS INSIDE PIPELINE, OWENS RIVER AQUEDUCT. William Mulholland supervised 5,000 workers in the six-year construction of the 233-mile Los Angeles Aqueduct. A bond election in 1910 provided the first public funds for the construction of ancillary municipal hydroelectric plants. All workers on the pipelines were under Mulholland's supervision; no private contractors undertook the work. Although consulting engineers feared a labor shortage, 4,000 tunnelers and diggers set to work in 1907 as city employees.

INTERNATIONAL AIR MEET, DOMINGUEZ FIELD. Dominguez Field was the site of the country's first international aviation meet from January 10 to 20, 1910. Historians Leonard and Dale Pitt reported, "The mayor declared a city holiday and the spectacle was attended by some 175,000 people." Spectators in the 2,000-seat grandstand saw Glenn Curtiss make a record-breaking 50-mile-per-hour flight. Pilot Louis Paulhan earned $50,000 for climbing to an altitude of 4,165 feet, and pioneer woman skydiver Georgia Broadwick parachuted from a hot air balloon.

ANGEL'S FLIGHT. For easy access up Bunker Hill to the fashionable mansions on its sides, Angel's Flight Railway was constructed. A short funicular, it traveled 335 feet with a 33-percent grade. The charge for a ride in 1910 was a penny. Bunker Hill was effectively leveled for redevelopment in 1970; Angel's Flight was moved a block away and then restored for service in 1995.

GENERAL VIEW OF SIXTH STREET, METHODIST CHURCH ON LEFT. Like many Eastern cities, Los Angeles built an array of downtown churches. First Methodist Church is shown in this 1910 postcard opposite Pershing Square Park, comfortable among its business block neighbors. The structure no longer exists.

DESTRUCTION OF THE TIMES BUILDING, FIRST AND BROADWAY. The bombing of the *Los Angeles Times* Building, shown on this 1910 postcard, attracted nationwide attention. In the Romanesque Revival style characteristic of many early downtown buildings, the structure was destroyed during a protracted labor struggle initiated by *Times* founder Harrison Gray Otis. The blast killed 20 men and injured 17 others.

DESTRUCTION OF TIMES BUILDING

THORPE OFFICE BUILDING

43

FOURTH AND MAIN STREETS. The Roman Revival bank shown in this postcard presents its elaborate temple-front entrances on both Fourth and Main. The intersection was the heart of Los Angeles' financial district in the first decade of the 20th century. The view shows the sharp incline of Fourth Street as it climbs toward Bunker Hill.

THE NORTH BROADWAY BRIDGE (BUENA VISTA VIADUCT). The first of the grand-style river bridges, the Buena Vista Viaduct, later renamed the North Broadway Bridge, was designed by leading Los Angeles architect Alfred F. Rosenheim in 1911. It featured hexagonal handrail balusters, pedestrian viewing bays, and 37-foot-tall paired Ionic entrance columns topped by a fanciful Doric entablature. (Regional History Collection/University of Southern California.)

THE PALACE THEATER ON BROADWAY. The Palace Theater, on Broadway between Sixth and Seventh Streets, was a 1911 design by architect G. Albert Lansburgh for the Orpheum Vaudeville Circuit. The palace enlivened the streetscape with its facade of polychrome terra-cotta arches by sculptor Domingo Mora. Lansburgh was the principal architect of theaters on the West Coast from 1900 to 1930.

TWO

BUILDING A CITY

OWENS RIVER AQUEDUCT, SERPENTINE PIPELINE. Pipes, siphons, tunnels, dams, and reservoirs advanced toward the city as relentlessly as the population burgeoned. "In the story of the aqueduct," wrote historian William K. Kahrl, "we confront the foundations of the modern metropolis of California."

OPPOSITE: OWENS RIVER AQUEDUCT FILLING THE BALDWIN HILLS RESERVOIR. Water from the Owens River Project spurred development in the city's outlying territories. Water from San Francisquito Dam filled a reservoir dug in the Baldwin Hills, south of downtown near present day Culver City.

FIFTH AND SPRING LOOKING WEST. This panoramic view taken in 1913 looking down on Fifth Street illustrates the local custom of landmarking buildings on the sides and rear with business names and services.

ENGINE NO. 30, LOS ANGELES FIRE DEPARTMENT. Old Fire Station 30, now the home of the African American Firefighter Museum, was established in 1913 to serve the Central Avenue community. The museum opened in 1997, the centennial of the induction of George W. Bright, Los Angeles' first African American firefighter, into the Los Angeles Fire Department. (Collection of the African American Firefighter Museum, Los Angeles.)

PRODUCE MARKET. The Central Avenue market was the main wholesale produce terminal for Los Angeles. Horses and wagons are still in use, but the postcard shows that trucks have begun to take over transport and distribution.

THE MONTENEGRO FAMILY. The language, culture, and customs of the Hispanic citizens of Los Angeles have been a continuous legacy to the city. Pride in family and tradition are evident in this portrait of the Montenegro family sons and daughters, who posed for a group portrait with their mother, Carmen, in 1917. (Shades of L.A. Collection/Los Angeles Public Library.)

VICTORY MEMORIAL BRIDGE—GLENDALE-HYPERION VIADUCT. Dedicated in 1919 as the Victory Memorial Bridge, Glendale-Hyperion Viaduct honored Los Angeles members of the American Expeditionary Forces in Europe during World War I. Austere conical towers and cast bronze light standards with globes shaped as candles echo the memorial theme of the bridge. Views north to the hills are of the Forest Lawn Memorial Park. (Security Pacific Collection/Los Angeles Public Library.)

OIL WELLS. The oil derricks pictured on this postcard were a familiar feature of the Los Angeles landscape in the first decades of the 20th century. Unsightly, noisy, and dirty, they were tolerated, if not loved, for their useful contribution to the culture of the car as well as the fortune of the city.

STATE THEATER. The State Theater on Broadway at Seventh Street was built in 1921 for the Loews Circuit. This structure's contribution to the elegance of the Broadway Theater district is the elaborate "silver platter" chased ornament above the ground story.

THE ACADEMY THEATER. An S. Charles Lee theater design, the Academy is a landmark in Streamline Moderne design. The rolling stucco cylinders of the base, glass block, ticket booth, and Art Deco lettering are meticulously crafted details of a composition directing focus to the tower. Its spiral fins were originally lit by blue neon tubes.

THE BADGER AVENUE (HENRY FORD) BRIDGE. Designed by famed engineer Joseph B. Strauss, the bridge connected Wilmington to the north side of Terminal Island in Los Angeles harbor. Strauss modernized the construction of the bascule, a variant of the medieval drawbridge. When opened in 1924, the structure stretched 760 feet across the Cerritos Channel with walkways for pedestrian traffic, rail lines for Santa Fe and Union Pacific freight traffic, and a street railway track. The structure was taken down in 1997 and replaced with a suspension bridge. (Collection of the Port of Los Angeles.)

BULLOCK'S WILSHIRE. In his new Wilshire Boulevard Store, John Bullock hired architects John and Donald Parkinson to design the quintessential Art Deco Zigzag Moderne design for shopping in the city of the future. Massing, materials, ornament, and the new building's copper-sheathed tower signaled a new approach in city retailing.

OPPOSITE: BULLOCK'S WILSHIRE, EXTERIOR MOTOR COURT. Bullock's Wilshire was designed to be easily entered from the rear porte cochere, where customers handed off their cars to a parking attendant. No expense was spared in the decoration of this motor entrance, which featured a ceiling mural entitled "The Spirit of Transportation."

LAFAYETTE PARK AND VIEW OF WILSHIRE BOULEVARD. Lafayette Park, a small, landscaped hollow of winding walks and lawns, features a Shakespeare Fountain and the decorative brick and stone Felipe deNeve Branch Library. This view looking west down Wilshire Boulevard shows the Town House and the tower of Bullock's Wilshire in the distance.

OPPOSITE: WILSHIRE BOULEVARD AND WESTERN AVENUE. This view of Wilshire Boulevard looking west shows the Pelissier Building and Wiltern Theater on the left. The Wiltern, a Los Angeles Art Deco Zigzag Moderne masterpiece with turquoise terra-cotta sheathing, was designed by Albert Lansburgh with an interior by Anthony B. Heinsbergen.

EARLY AIRPLANE PASSENGER. This happy flyer, who had just returned from a spin on one of the many hour-long pleasure flights that Angelenos could take to experience the thrills of flight, marked the occasion with two snapshots mailed to a friend. On the back of this picture, the message reads, "Here I am just as we landed; the pilot helping me off the plane. Just a small step." (Collection of Glen Dean Jones, Riverside.)

SUBWAY TERMINAL BUILDING. The elegance and architectural distinction of the Beaux Arts Subway Terminal Building, designed by Los Angeles architects Schultz and Weaver in 1926, declared the importance of transportation to Los Angeles.

OPPOSITE: OPENING OF LOS ANGELES SUBWAY. In 1926 the Pacific Electric Railway began an ambitious plan for a Los Angeles subway to provide rapid access to downtown from the west side and San Fernando Valley. A tunnel was built in 1925 from First Street and Glendale Boulevard to an underground station at Fourth and Hill Streets below the Subway Terminal Building.

THE BILTMORE HOTEL FACING PERSHING SQUARE. This view from Pershing Square Park looks northwest toward the Biltmore. Constructed in 1928, the Biltmore Hotel soon became and remains today the most important historic downtown hotel. The E-shaped, 13-story structure has eclectic revival architectural details with white terra-cotta at the top and ground story and red-brick facing. Balconies are a feature of the upper floors. Off the lobby is the Fifth Street Corridor, which has traditionally functioned as an interior shopping street or galleria. The ceilings of many of the ground-floor meeting rooms were painted by Los Angeles artist-decorator Anthony Heinsbergen.

MINES AIRFIELD. In 1928, the city of Los Angeles leased 640 acres of agricultural land near present day Westchester to build an oiled landing strip and two hangars to house 20 planes each. The small airfield expanded throughout the 1930s and became the Los Angeles International Airport after World War II. This official photograph documents the competitor's positions at the National Air Races on September 15, 1928.

THE RICHFIELD BUILDING. The shimmering black terra-cotta walls with gold-strip accents of the Art Deco Moderne Richfield building symbolized the "black gold" of oil. Considered the finest example of Los Angeles' Art Deco Moderne, it was designed in 1928 by Morgan, Walls, and Clements. The company demolished the structure in 1972 to make way for two larger buildings on the site.

SPRING STREET, "WALL STREET OF THE WEST." The five-story Moderne gray granite building in the foreground was built in 1929 as the Pacific Coast Stock Exchange.

THE TOWN HOUSE. The Town House on Wilshire Boulevard opposite Lafayette Park was a grand, full-service residential hotel with a pool and tennis courts. Built at Los Angeles' original height limit of 13 stories, the hotel had an underground garage for its tenant's cars, an innovation in 1928 that reflected the development of Wilshire Boulevard as a district of elite businesses, churches, and residences dependent on the automobile. The structure is listed on the California Register of Historic Places. Bullock's Wilshire is prominent on the south side of the boulevard.

CURTIS WRIGHT FLYING SERVICE. Grand Central Air Terminal opened in Glendale in 1929 and was the premier airport in Southern California until the advent of jets in 1955. The first transcontinental flight from Southern California to New York originated at Grand Central with Charles A. Lindbergh as pilot. Curtiss Flying Service operated the airport and a technical school for repair and maintenance as well as modification of planes and engines. Maintenance Building, Hanger No. 1, a handsome example of California Mission Revival style, no longer exists, although the former airport terminal building and tower remain.

THREE

TOWARD THE MODERN ERA

PERSHING SQUARE FOUNTAIN. This view shows the center of Pershing Square Park c. 1930. Water flows over the sculptured figures of four cherubs into a large pool. In this era, the park featured brick paving, palm-shaded walks, large banana plants, and wood benches.

THE MIRACLE MILE. The Miracle Mile was a prestigious shopping center on Wilshire Boulevard west of downtown. Developer A. W. Ross conceived this portion of Wilshire Boulevard as an Art Deco linear retail center of prestige department stores offering free parking and saving the buying public a trip downtown.

THE SOUTHERN CALIFORNIA EDISON BUILDING (ONE BUNKER HILL) UNDER CONSTRUCTION. The elaborate steel frame of the 12-story Edison Building shows its futuristic massing and one-story pavilion entrance addressing the northwest corner of Grand and West Fifth Streets. Built in 1930–1931, the Art Deco building integrates art and architecture with lobby murals and entrance relief panels depicting hydroelectric energy, light, and power.

CLIFTON'S CAFETERIA, SIXTH AND OLIVE STREETS. Each Clifton's Cafeteria had its own theme. The Pacific Seas branch on Sixth and Olive Street in downtown Los Angeles featured flowing waterfalls and indoor humidity for exotic tropical plants. Civic reformer Clifford Clinton arrived in Los Angeles during the Great Depression. With the motto "pay what you can," he opened the first of his chain of seven cafeterias in July 1931, providing free meals to those who could pay nothing.

LOS ANGELES THEATER. The grandest example of theater decoration in downtown Los Angeles, the Los Angeles Theater, was designed in 1931 by S. Charles Lee, regarded as the master of movie-palace expressionism. Classical grandeur and Baroque ornamentation were applied with the utmost exuberance.

LOS ANGELES THEATER INTERIOR.
Architect Lee is said to have
modeled the opulent interior of
the Los Angeles after the Hall of
Mirrors in Versailles. A crystal
fountain was placed at the head of
the grand staircase. The theater
had a restaurant and a ballroom on
the lower levels.

WILSHIRE AND VERMONT LOOKING WEST TOWARD BULLOCK'S WILSHIRE. Despite the operation of an enormous public transportation system of street cars and buses, the car soon became the most popular mode of travel. The results were predictable: congestion, traffic jams, accidents, and parking tickets. The unforeseen consequences of economic growth brought about by the car were the city's decentralization and the development of suburban housing.

GOODRICH BUILDING. This beautifully maintained composition of lawn and trees in an industrial setting demonstrates the commitment that early builders made to landscape. Land was not a scarce commodity and water was imported in abundance. Community spirit demanded that the streetscape and building grounds be cultivated.

CARPENTERS DRIVE-IN. In the 1930s, drive-in architecture symbolized the spirit of the city: hungry motion, machines, and modernism. Carpenter's Drive-In at Wilshire Boulevard and Western Avenue combined the comfort and privacy of eating in the car with the fun of going out. Typical of late-1930s drive-ins, it had a simple three-element program: the central kitchen and order area, canopy, and the neon-lit tower that functioned as a sign, diverting cruising drivers to the scene.

St. Bernard Café. St. Bernard Café advertised itself on this 1938 postcard as a "Tyrolese" restaurant. Another draw to patrons and their families were the stuffed dogs in the windows.

UNION STATION PASSENGER TERMINAL, ALAMEDA AND SUNSET BOULEVARDS, LOOKING WEST TOWARD CITY HALL. Historians Leonard and Dale Pitt describe Union Passenger Terminal as "the last of the great American railroad stations." Built in 1939 by a consortium of the city's architects headed by Donald B. Parkinson, the station comprises a group of one-story, stucco, tile-roofed buildings dominated by a 135-foot observation and clock tower. The structure is a highly artistic rendering of Spanish Colonial Revival architecture with a Moderne sensibility. The handsome interior has a 52-foot-tall ceiling, marble floor, tall arched windows facing gardens on two sides, and superb California tile ornamentation.

UNION STATION INTERIOR. The decorative details in this interior space—patterned ceiling, extensive use of tile, and decorative metal grill work—work in harmony with decorative use of architectural structure revealed in piers and arches. This unity of detail and structure is a fundamental design principle apparent throughout the station complex.

UNION AIR TERMINAL BURBANK, C. 1940. In 1928, Boeing Air Transport Company developed Boeing Air Field in Burbank in a sandy loam vineyard with giant oak and eucalyptus trees. A dry riverbed ran through the center of the property. In 1930, the airport was dedicated as United Airport, heralding the company-sponsored airline. It opened on Memorial Day with a three-day air show featuring exhibition flights of Boeing P-12 pursuit planes and Keystone bombers. In 1934, the facility was renamed Union Air Terminal, Burbank.

BROADWAY BETWEEN FIRST AND SECOND STREETS. This view of Broadway *c.* 1940 shows a solid and prosperous business and civic street with a mixed low-rise–high-rise streetscape.

SECOND AND BROADWAY. Broadway between Second and Third Streets is captured here at a lull in the usually bustling traffic pattern. Overhead trolley and street railway lines show that the intersections was an important transfer point. Upper Broadway lacked major department stores or large office buildings, so congestion increased as the traveler moved south.

CANNERY WORKERS, TERMINAL ISLAND. Prior to relocation in internment camps at the beginning of World War II, a thriving colony of Japanese Americans lived and worked on Terminal Island in the Port of Los Angeles. Jean Watasuki Houston, in her memoir *Farewell to Manzanar*, recalls that Terminal Island's cannery workers reported to the plant whenever the blast of the whistles alerted them to the arrival of the boats. "One for Stokely's; two for Van Camp's," brought workers down to the processing sheds day or night. (Security Pacific Collection/Los Angeles Public Library.)

BROADWAY AND TWELFTH STREET AFTER SNOWSTORM. Snow in Los Angeles in February 1948 was unusual enough to warrant the creation of this postcard, presumably to send back to the folks in colder climates to show that it wasn't always sunny and warm in Southern California.

HOLLYWOOD FREEWAY. The Hollywood Freeway, completed in 1948, ran from downtown Los Angeles through Hollywood to the San Fernando Valley, which was then experiencing exponential post–World War II population growth. The road was engineered with four lanes in each direction, functional and banked curves, paved shoulders, and extended access lanes. A true freeway, it had few landscaping or parkway features.

123

RICHFIELD SERVICE STATION WITH FULL SERVICE ATTENDANTS. The Richfield Company chose an imposing Classical Revival style to shelter the pumps and attendants that checked under the hood of this motorist's fine 1948 Chevy Fleetline two-door sedan.

LOS ANGELES EXAMINER BUILDING. Commissioned in 1915 by William Randolph Hearst and designed by Julia Morgan, the Examiner Building featured Mission arches, loggias, ornamental iron, and plaster work, and an impressive lobby with patterned-tiled floors and elaborate friezes. When the building was complete, Hearst wrote, "I am glad to note the building combines with its efficient qualities those pleasing traits reminiscent of an architecture that is identified with the beautiful and romantic history of Los Angeles and California."

Arcadia Publishing is the leading local history publisher in the United States. With more than 3,000 titles in print and hundreds of new titles released every year, Arcadia has extensive specialized experience chronicling the history of communities and celebrating America's hidden stories, bringing to life people, places, and events from the past. To discover the history of other communities across the nation, please visit:

www.arcadiapublishing.com

Customized search tools allow you to find regional history books about the town where you grew up, the cities where your friends and relatives live, the town where your parents met, or even that retirement spot you've been dreaming of. The Arcadia website also provides history lovers with exclusive deals, advanced notice of new titles, e-mail alerts of author events, and much more.